T0094573

THE LOVING DETAIL
OF THE LIVING & THE DEAD

Also by Eleni Sikelianos

The Loving Detail
of the Living & the Dead

POEMS
Eleni
Sikelianos

COFFEE HOUSE PRESS
Minneapolis 2013

Coffee House Press books are available to the trade through our primary distributor, Consortium Book Sales & Distribution, cbsd.com. For personal orders, catalogs, or other information, write to: Coffee House Press, 79 Thirteenth Avenue NE, Suite 110, Minneapolis, MN 55413.

Coffee House Press is a nonprofit literary publishing house. Support from private foundations, corporate giving programs, government programs, and generous individuals helps make the publication of our books possible. We gratefully acknowledge their support in detail in the back of this book.

Good books are brewing at coffeehousepress.org

LIBRARY OF CONGRESS CATALOGING-IN-PUBLICATION DATA
Sikelianos, Eleni.
The loving detail of the living & the dead : poems /
by Eleni Sikelianos.
p. cm.
ISBN 978-1-56689-324-4 (pbk.)
I. Title.
PS3569.I4128L68 2013
811'.54—DC23
2012037718

PRINTED IN THE UNITED STATES

a bit of fire from the world pools in the ear
& burns there

Bird & Meat Subject

My little bird & meat subject
  little human eye unhinging like a door
    I'm addressing you & you are the title
        my little bird-&-meat

                  The skin slips off by a strange arrangement

  like a boat that begins to take water
  before the storm —
      the words
in my throats

      once sure as cream

spinning the human voice
around the atom, cracks it

my little bird-&-meat
(holds out her hand, bends her fingers), say hello
to this time-eating spider

Finally, the Shadow — *Sw.t* —
(inside the hem)

                                        world the black — world the blank
                                                          —margin

there is no —
          no place —
    no place where the —
the dead animals
          hover
here
in this fringe
that is
earth

lost time collects in the creases

          bone-crushed dust off a minute
          dust it off! mantel of time!

we arrive & there's a corpse of an hour, what happened
here?

★
    say: by my heart's wish I constructed a city —

          at the foot of Mt. Muzri
in the countryside surrounding Nineveh —
    and gave its name as Dur-Sharrukin

2

(had a double who did my work for me, mowed the lawn, did the dishes, little
clay figure; lost it, lost my shedu in the river)

And in the Upper Paleolithic, we found ourselves
wild onager, red deer, sheep, goat, fox, gazelle, pig, cow, bird, clam, crab, tortoise
and snail.
We ate them all.

Ate chrysanthemums, ate nasturtiums, every blossom, grass, anther and nut

Flower how hun-
gry you make me   swim swim
to the river in asthmatic   sun-
light   collect wild seeds there

By the river, the corpse of an hour, it asks us: what happened here

★

  say: we saw history
the rocks and grasses sang themselves into houses
rubble turned to hut
we wandered *the ruthless, splendid labyrinths* laid out in gold,
blue and green: tangles of trees, water, weather, animal and sand

Married the river, married the rock, gold dug out was the dowry
and soon the hem of a train, steam-trail rising like wedding-dress dust

Built roads, built bridges, little plastic dolls with eyes that open and shut;
seeded clouds and nanocrystals; turned the heavens; made
infrared imaging capabilities on CRYSTAL reconnaissance satellites
made the Military Black World

Soon so many persons made so many person-things
till it seemed all that was left of the world was human

How quickly sound travels through these acidified oceans!
How quickly we folded spring into summer!
Constructed bio-available time!

Ate the quail, woodcock, the turtle, fattened liver, the veal calf

our tongues decaying
one by one
near the teeth   by my heart's
orifact, Mercury mouth
Walk away

★

Like atmospheric lace
dust-dress of the world never settles   And inside the hem
winter steals a mouse

4

Charlene

Everyone is the weather of our home star
Enclose the future in your liver
With the audacity of a jewel trap
The future where there's nothing left
    Charlene
your hair was
a tall girl, big girl   blonde as cigarette smoke
You had a boat by the river, little boat tied to the banks
a wooden ship of luxury because   freedom
is   You could float away, come home
               float away, come
                          home
without the weight of your own actions
ripping the organs out of your body
Charlene
the body holds the vowels like a baby arming the "O"
sideways U the future shape of the liver
blue U liver
why U
Charlene
Kidney's emerald
Light blue Charlene
Eat your bowl of money

Someone photographs the hands trembling in black air

Skin on a Dime

Charlene puts skin on a dime
leather on a dollar
food on her face
money on the table

Charlene
I'm a homemade monster
& you're a homemade oyster

Your circle has a poppy hole

The Human Portfolio

to express milk, like expressing a feeling
     the feeling of milk
         my little lactating portfolio
  pressed above the ribs
     should you open it find

I'm happy for that horse
     happy horse (human horse), learned to sing

little human bird and horse in the bush
learning all that can be done with a seed, a word, & a handkerchief

  that a breath is a beast of a species
     snouting out
  snarling in

body
the world's convert

world
the body's accomplice

I mean any body
ho!

then a cloud creaks in the wind or is popped with a silver needle

Some Assemblies of the Past & Present (see how it rises)

I

My goddess is stoned
in a translucent pose
in a tense that is not past
her shoulder
lights the road

notice
who hides in her heel —
tap tap (toe
on the curb) — people

in a dark

corner of
bone

II

There's a softbox in my window
A little edge where eternity bleeds at the back of the throat-blur

Thirsty traveler,
the future's out back hatcheting flamingoes from gone ice

> *Are you monstering me?*
> *Goddess, are you?*

Even peas in the garden show time's shadow right
on the ground so

Go on: Adapt yourself now
Reader, grow new time

The foot soon forgets its path through the soft heather but the heart
so spectacularly charged with mitochondria remembers its mother

III

Where was I trying to go?
I found myself with the knockout mice on the loading docks
just after the delivery.
They've knocked a few
of her genes out
like knocking on her future
physical door or
as you would   teeth
from a   head.

IV

Before us, this pile of scraps, this
pile of trash, this pile of
American minutes
dressed up in Chinese clothing

Among the forests of my many-folded

(hours unfolding)
see how the air rises, sky-kissing,
a bonfire of energy spending itself in blue

Let yourself be that way, Goddess.

It's like putting your sky in a lost place
like letting a pirate borrow your sword.

From her shoulder's light slip
                              loose   coins   —

It's all that matters in the world.

I purse the red throat of a loon.

v (*The Ba, the Ka, the Akh, the Name, and the Shadow*)

When you come out of the pose

Do you come out heavy?
Do you come out light?
Too pride-hustled?
Too sleek?

My human-headed bird, bird-
shaped human
my *ba*, face of gold like the goddess's
shoulder and
skin
Fly off to bash in the sun

but come home tonight divested
of that dress I recognize
clothed in some animal
I don't —
Still

I know you and I know your names

Your face is face
in a translucent pose —

See how it rises, sky-kissing

see how it rises, sky-kissing

Actual Sky

Scene: *We have finally done away with the robot killers pursuing us (Buckminster Fuller is a teenager with shoulder-length shiny black hair drawing Dymaxion houses in red air) (When there's nowhere left to live we'll live there) Consciousness is the last thing ejected, like a purged river the citizenry had neglected.*
Outside this room, a storm is gathering to ionize the sky.
These are my words.

Like a weed, consciousness floats spaceward in a tear-shaped capsule.
Who made this crystalline drop of saline water?

Who made this mistake?
Nature did.
Made the Mind and the Trees grow too fast.
Made Lord Swirl-it-Shit.
A lignin ignition, a coal-forest fact ready to fire.

What grabs what's hand to fall to earth as mercury. What
does the tear care if you cry it?

what won't douse the fire

Nerve-wires Run Bullet Trains through Lit Tunnels

I learned the use of
        the deep vessel

   the *in* body the *out* body

our demotic bodies shattering inside
   our bodies

a dramatic octopus with ribbons

First we draw a semi-person
   then you color it in

        the purest
             monsters   /

mirrors   plus the first O the mouth
makes out of the womb   and blonde
light streaking past when the last

vowel trips   and scatters
across the room   /   the moon   (O)

Thank You for My Machu Picchu / The Container Schema / God in That Image

Do you believe God was made
  I mean man
    do you believe was made
        in that image?

No, man was made in the image of a flower
& then the flower got fucked up.

—What flower?
—(what storm?)

Woman was made in the image of a nest
       then the bones began to congeal
like toothpicks seeking
the mother-tree.

What about the sky?

In relation to the self?

           What shadow overtook me
           out of /   birth, a shapeless   wound.

At dawn, the hounds crawled back to bed.

—What are you talking about?

The history of man.

Charlene is talking about

Thundersnow, and the way a man can smell like a moon, a woman
like a man; the smell is her shadow; sound is

A woman a Swede I know once walked to Lapland from the airport
    in midnight sun, four hours on the open road with another four
    to go, she finally flagged down some birders who took her
    close but not home

                a figure groping for its family
                a description foraging for its face

People — whose love is just the right size
    for their bodies, & never breaks out

People — whose love is too big for their bodies & comes busting
        out through the bones & the skin

                a specimen in pursuit of its kind, of its kin

But Charlene: is she brown or blonde or black

When I posted the shadow of myself
                    my herself
was her shadow blanched white?

An And and Thought

I found an and
    and thought

what if this were America, this room?

I found an if and
if it were France?

Let us go on cultivating these fields of error

Found a so and so I found myself
in Colorado
    in a havoc of bees, fallen and frozen

I found a what and what
to do with it?

I found a to and pointed it but did not pull the trigger

Found an or or
an ear I
    couldn't hear which

Who took my not and sentenced it
to palinodes in corners of the womb?

To live live lively
A dog licking stars

I found an in, an on, an as, and
knotted them together

To live live wounded as one who fell in the morning and
    hurt her knee

I fondled the the I
found, and the a

A beautiful painful grammar walks through my brain

What if it were
the rifle in the human blind?

I Too Want to Sleep in America Tonight

I am full of nostalgia tonight
  like a sootbag filled with rocks
my hometown's shining behind me
  in the avocados' glistening skins
The lemon's electricity socks

my leg is starting to break
but my feet are not breaking
so I can walk

but my stomach is starting to break
around my mouth
  says it's nighttime
where I forget my teeth
& my teeth-shine

my ankle is breaking but my thumb is not
breaking
around my thought

bone particles hover inside the wrist
like a luminous halo of feeling the flesh once hid

The life fact shines like loving-oil all over the body

Anatomical Eclipse — Charlene's

fingernail brushes the curve
                                    of earth

& the wrist rotates there

Around it oxygenates, a
                                    haloed bracelet of air

Her rib-bones make speeches
                    to a bird who heard
                                    her egg snap in the high nest

  who next converses with the president:

The small thumb-bone floats
            in a crimson sea   believing its gene pool to be a
                            seahorse's kin

Her stomach a staging ground for hymnals

and the stealth of the inner thigh
            how she ties ribbons around
                    the future how she hides
                a nation's intentions in the flesh

(I'm asking her to change the world.)

  Of course she is a goddess.
  She's a living woman.
  She's mon semblable.

She has some chickens.
She's my friend.

Her fingers glitter with some animal time had wounded.

Verb / Verbatim (Eva's first told dream)

What's mamma do
you're back, you came back from the snow

Did you been in the snow
  when I was dreaming about you?
      You carried the horses
          on your back, you held them
tight all the way from Denver, you carried
        the snow on your back

What's mamma do —
I'm sleeping *and* I'm dying

The foot soon forgets its path through the soft heather

Black-Out Fabric — What I Found There

They had long dreamed of an ideal black that absorbs all colors while reflecting no light.

      (in the light my fact unfurled :)

Can you see a difference a
  darker difference
       between this black and that?
The darkest fabric ever found was found to be
Made by man. Upon that carpet I found

    a patch of carbon nanotube grass, a loosely packed
    forest full of nanoscale gaps
    and holes to collect and trap
    light. Tried a picnic upon that scrap, but soon discovered

    how random are the surfaces.
    My tincture thought it was a bird
    my golgi got all confused
    (what do golgi do? sent the macro-
        molecule package to the wrong parts — what hinter-
          lands a hand can grip)
    : my eurkaryotes cried so dusky
    : my coinciding eye set out seeking its companionship
      but came back black
    : my corresponding ribonucleic haze lazing around the dark nucleotides
    : passing through its lumens
my mars mistook itself for sky
    : my clouds retrieved themselves from black

(a good nut of a nucleus decoupling the cytoskeleton)
: my two bullets flew by night
life-to-life, debt-to-debt, all tries
to undo its ties. All rise.
(a twist in the basement membranes and their gut-like helices)
my tooth at the hardened crumb just so
(the cell or the will kills the beam, 99.955%)
: my empire lists its genomic odes
: my hedgerow escrowed : my blood released its weathermen
— a corpse was found the story asked what is this stinking history
(another girl is murdered)
my wind did wind around her bones :
sunlight laces straight her ribs :
: my bomb illuminating my hand and bird
(another war unfolded)
: my beast-head asleep on the rock
: my human legs in yellow light
: my fact decayed in the light

Instructions

I
Make a poem
that descends in the mirror

then comes back out

II
make a poem of an animal (say, gazelle)
that you can never catch

let it bound & disappear & bound

let it be both bound by and
escaping the rooms of the poem

III
make a poem that eats itself

IV
make a poem that aerates the situation
that situates the self
let a body lost in consciousness
keep finding itself there

Mary Wore a Red Dress

Where did Mary wear
her red dress, where did Mary
go? To the corner, for
milk, in the milk-grey
morning light, Mary. Mary will not go
forever, she will not wear
the red dress
forever, she is in motion : moving
just between these light frames, she jumps
like old oil on a hot griddle, Mary in
a velvet past
that tatters as it moves
toward me, that's how time goes : how will Mary
Mary get to the future
What is the future, it's a past
place, tattered
red
red flag in scattered light
where hawk has been, to put a child
to sleep, where hawk has gone
to see a child sleep, what hawk has heard, Mary over the Aquiville River
Mary of the blue air around
Mary of the milky past, child of my own
hawk-light, child of grass

when it says "fragile" above a body sleeping in the doorway

Inside the Dome

What pleasure seeds we found inside the dome!
a cracked nut, a crystal home, a cold body, a squirrel's domain

The memory house too airy & blown out to hold more

Tagged the memory & sent it off to scavenge: we need more
rocks in this loving pile

We soon defoliated the feeling & sent it back;
it grew new shoots under the UV lights

We bound all the memories of mothers together in one bundle but
the white thread dissolved like sutures
the thread decayed & then we couldn't tell
what belonged to whom, whom to what

I could see I'd never known this mother [person] [father] before

Where was the memory of my grandmother?

Howling in the hall.
Dark hell-hall.

She's so angry, someone said.

Wouldn't you be too if you were a lost memory?

She scratched the metal of her surface on me
It came off nickel, a corrosive reminiscence shedding atoms

All the mad seeds of memory seemed to fall near eternity
All the glad ones, too, bumping into the heart's soft walls

Milk, Pebble, Pear

The shadow falls from the glass of milk like a ghost, another
   pools beneath the pear
A pebble hovers in the mind and the mind's hand
(Everything belongs to the brain)

I shall hear a shift in the pear and the pear's gear, a break in the time span
Like the tinkle of smashing glass
I moved to the other side of the room, & there a glass of milk
The same glass of milk; it was like waking up a second time
: Name three things in the room

the context is a table
it holds quite a few things up
let the body settle
this rock traveled to get here

   when time breaks :
   like a glass of milk with a crack :
   a milky trickle flows as if
   a miniscule fissure at the volcano's base : the volcano
   at the back of a baby's mouth :
             mouth

               of time
            milk :
               of time
                   flows :

       flaws out

In the Airport

A man called Dad walks by
then another one does. Dad, you say
and he turns, forever turning, forever
being called. Dad, he turns, and looks
at you, bewildered, his face a moving
wreck of skin, a gravity-bound question
mark, a fruit ripped in two, an animal
that can't escape the field.

Shadow Zoo

About the bars of light
across the trees

About the shadows blocking
each trunk into a geometric

stage for more shadow play
About the depth the eye

perceives through the limbs
when my shadow touched itself

      torched it

where was your shadow?

The deer wearing theirs across the hillside, the wasps
crashing through the windows, sun-drunk, stormy blobs shadowing
                          the pane

The past was a shadow running backwards, wearing itself
      in a cloak we couldn't see
                   The future seen
in the deer trimming the grass then wearing their shadows down to nubs

A river shadows this room: backside of the specific electricity surging through
      the house

For the blind man who gained sight everything was flat, he had to learn to see
the shadow fruit the seemingly tasteless shadow fruit giving everything depth

Throw your shadow on the cave wall, then charcoal in the horse's throat

You can make a man ill by stabbing it

and wouldn't his eyes be filled with darkness
(he thought in the light there'd be no more shadow)
(he stepped there)
and wouldn't his eyes hurt
and wouldn't he turn and flee
by the rough steep path if
someone dragged you
into sunlight

The cracked atom, its shadow like a mosquito hovering over the lawn
The silos hugging spent fuel cast theirs in the background

who will hold fast
who will strike, who will wound   will sound   your shadow
if your shadow falls on the stone and the demon of the stone draws it

At noon you may lose your shadow

If
a hyena steps on it in moonlight
a dog on a roof can be dragged by its echo (as if by rope)

The Minuteman missile is maintained on alert in an unmanned, hardened under-
ground launch facility approximately 80 feet deep, 12 feet in diameter, and covered by a
100-ton blast door which is blown off prior to missile launch

"You are the shadow at the back, looming
                    like a trace"

Bury a woman's shadow under the foundation stone, or find
the first animal that comes along

(Beware the shadow-trader who deals the shadows the builder needs)

These are the things that detain the soul in the mind:
Shadows, flames, trees, columns, dolls, pools, children, Polaroids, carbon, waste

Bluff and counterbluff thrown across the oceans streak their shadows sea-bottom and

if your shadow lit
lit up
if your shadow were aflame
the tip of the matchstick
burning the body back
to its shadow
the mind holding it there

She wears a wedge of shadow like a pendant on a chain dangling
   in the shadowy triangle above the heart
      to the right if you are facing her
      to the left if you are her

He said:
First, shadows, then reflections in water and in all close-packed, smooth,
and shiny materials, and everything of that sort, if you understand

of the visible, put the originals of these images, namely the animals around us,
all the plants, and the whole class of manufactured things

He answered:
Consider them put

Add my shadow
It happens in black & white   and
Earth's umbra derelicted across the moon

What I learned in this town today:
a giraffe's extra big heart keeps it from passing out
once it lifts its big face on its long neck back up from the grass that
hides its shadows
at the root

unstitch my shadow
shadow giraffe
I stitch it back

unstitch
my purpose, stitching, trimming, which is
to walk upon the grass and walk upon the shadow grass

Song: Wake with William

I'd like to wake with William Blake
his head upon my pillow
He'd turn to me & say to thee
How the light is yellow!
The mind is gold & we are old
& now we're getting older
The body is violet, purple, & blue
Your feet, bright, the
darkest blackness out there
black hole the body
black hole the body
every side of glory

Little boy who makes haunted vowels
his head upon my pillow
from sleep's hollow
a giant U escapes becomes
a deep sea ghost a giant
squid U
U my palatine

black hole the glory
every side of body

stake it down   with the little proper copper love nails

The Clouds in Heaven

In hell clouds are made of wood or
stone they hit our heads, the ground They cannot hold
rain or sleet or snow
Charlene said musing — In
heaven —   you know about the clouds
in heaven   They are the palinodes
of hell's stone clouds   They are
still loud   Sometimes the edges
of a hell cloud & a heaven one
will graze each other & make
a terrible laughing like paper thunder

Of, if the cloud is destroyed by laughter
If, of the voice razed by thunder
Under, if the heaven is taken by surprise [its britches]
Whether, if the hell is heaped asunder or torn by numbers

When a cloud creaks in the wind or
is popped with a silver needle like a red balloon
then a cloud may catch and tear a root out by its trees

And clouds, I believe, have waves inside that make a noise
of the kind that wavelings make in water, sobbing up and down the shore

Dream Event: My Husband & The Devil

Now I know that was the devil or one of his minions scuttling up and down his ropes like a gleefully malignant, worn-out spider. Black stockings with knotty mendings, black pointed hat flopping down, pointy buckled shoes — everything *on* that devil was spiky — chin, hat, eyes, toes. Why did he have you tied to the top of the clock tower like a chastised fly-in-danger? I had to find the missing element to save you; I believe it was a piece of time — a little knob or rope of it, a bit of illuminating temporal genetic code. Once I got up there to you and fit the missing string of time in, it would light up, multicolored like an enormous Lite-Brite. But I couldn't distract the devil long enough before I woke. Why were you, your you-soul, why was my self-soul — why were we being held captive by a time-devil dressed in black like an ancient undertaker? The only way to free ourselves was illumination, light, and color, so please draw this clarified sky for me.

The Humans Attract All the Light of Destiny to Themselves

for Akilah

That the father sleeps in the house of his son's killer
That the father kisses his son's killer's man-killing hands
That the gods who agree to kill the man preserve the man's body
That we know the killer will die but he does not die in the poem
That I know I will die but I do not die in the poem
That it is the man killed who tells us the killer will die
That the killer will be killed by the man-he-has-killed's brother
That we know the brother will die
That these deaths do not happen in the poem
That my friend will die, and it did happen in a poem
That we know the mother will die
The daughter will die before or after the mother
The father will die the son will die before or after the mother
The mother will die the sister
When after death does it migrate from *her body* to *the body*?
Is this the cult of death? (living)
The killer wishes to eat the man he kills raw
The man he kill's mother wishes to eat the killer raw, to "sink [her] teeth in his liver"
To have a heart erupting with slaughter
To be placed on a bier with slaughtered beasts after you have been slaughtered
That you go on a manhunt to kill a man
That you kill a man or a woman or a child in a cave, in a compound, in a café, in
    a forest, on the plains
That the gods do not preserve the body
That you cannot wrap your arms around the ghost

Beehive the Mind (the dead woman answers the question)

Eyes
closed like blackened
flowers Howling mouth What have you
found *Hallways*
empty with air Abraham
Lincoln down with you in
the tall-short space of
the dead   low-ceilinged
high-ceilinged dead Abraham's
dead hat Did you carry
your dead life with you
little tiger   limp sack in your
arms the form of your life
ghost of your life in your dead
arms What did you learn out
there in the sands of the dead

I learned the old loving detail of the breath
That this crystal has tissue
This rock has flesh
How to dispel a storm with the first morning light
How to mirror the spot-
light Life-
lit like the G-
spot We don't beehive human minds
to explode an atom
Everything here is
exploded atoms

Her fable

and we came to a shed in the woods
(that's how I found you)
keeping time to the cacophonic flesh
I reach without thinking for the flashlight we kept
If I were to live in a little orange tent by the side of the freeway
it would be too cold at night to cry
a baby deer cries like a big crow
Charlene cries like a baby deer

Charlene said

There are actually two heavens
& one's called Hell & one's
called Heaven
& they speak to each other
through a megaphone
& in one we make ideas
& in the other we destroy them
I make an idea in Heaven
Hell destroys it
I make an idea in Hell
Guess what Heaven does

Black crust of night on my face
Mouth blowing down a teapot spout
Down on Diversey Street
When you were wrestling with the phone book
You tried to call that Latvian woman
But she was an Estonian ghost
She spoke
my language:
Tapetum lucidum (bright tapestry): that mirror that
makes a cat's eyeshine in the dark

fingers glitter with some animal time had wounded

Essay: The Living Leave the Dead

"for thought cannot journey through time without meeting death on the way"
for Poppy

The mind caresses the body, lingering
 caresses a shoulder, a sinew

The mind is loath to leave the body, kissing
  its frames, its skins

The lymph circulates, the mind follows
  its eddies & flows
The mind worries the body's muscles & bones

Now the body worries the mind.

There lies the body, the mind is over it
 a settling wind

Where shall it go?
(Body has shut up shop. Closed
  the shutters; liver, kidneys, closed.)

How lucky,
we don't have to answer the telephone after we're dead.

★

A living part, the part of me that was my live uncle (Poppy), like an organ, has died.

*

what parts of the body the soul *doesn't mean*

*

Replacing the family organs that sleep in the body like loving, licking ghosts, a new ghost organ comes to live in my body.
My Live-Poppy-Kidney goes crystal & bright, beaded, with an inside light. Luminating; my new dead ghost-kidney replaces it now that his body is dead (lymph still circulating).

—It doesn't *replace*, it just changes itself
—O.K.

—*Get* the *shapes* of the dead and the living we carry inside.
—O.K.

Carrying our own living ghost inside
        our dead ghost comes later & lives
        in a different way

The little animal body
the little animal hood around
my daughter shining —

her pretty live animal ghost
still living

Her fingers like little luminous
golden ghost chopsticks
snapping clacking   the air
Neck holding up all that head
consciousness like a silk
scarf stuffed inside an apple

pull the scarf out of the hat (head) &
let it loose on the air   see it float   see it fly
                  like a silk wave rolling
over the sky   earth   circling

                          just the
way the sun is round & light   or the earth
is   round   round tremble & light

Skin of fire we swim through

              I send you off

hairy skin of fire a   fuzz, a fur - fire
        a fur skinning the   right angle of the letter A
     we slide down it, we climb up
                          skin of the self — fire — a buzz
              skin of the world — fuzz —

I think, or maybe that's backwards:

                    somewhere we get burned
                        anyway
                    a
                    fire fuzz

that is like a firefly melting its light into the night &
        bursting its skin

    or the redemptive properties of a stone shedding atoms

Other letters appeared to me, skinless
        & skinned
    at the self's earliest minute   she said
        B   ablaze a scaffolding dangling ropes
                                It folded
into the wormhole, which was colorful (I thought,
    "Crayola"   the singularity is full of smudges
I thought   the soul's a vortex, the still center of   a tornado & around it, swirling is
melted color & black

            so this is the form's soul   alphabet   soul's form
                    which is it which is a
                        tornado its
                        eye hole

I could not find the z.

{Coda} {Ferocious the}

ferocious the
little mechanical suns
open their lungs

&kick

Charlene binds a Leopard & leads a Mule (sayings & deeds)

For moss is the tree's spangled dress
and rain moistens the eyes as we look
and the first "s" in *grass* is its curves
and the second "s" its blades in wind
For green brightens the eyes & lights the heart
and "g" dangles as the instance between tadpole and frog
and a red truck goes by which is a thought from god speeding toward light
and I am collecting the world for you
and now I am disassembling it
and a rain puddle is god's mirror
and the trees, what lovely devices for god's tresses
and god's coiffure what god what good

More Charlene Sayings & Deeds

for the ribbon grass is god's strap & light catcher
for it is a soft belt that teases air
      & air teases it
for its expression of grace is a light puff of smoke disguised as grassflower
for the expression of green follows the heart & lights on the leaves
for the wind is a kissing in its gentlest divulgence
but a lashing when excited or enraged
the geranium's blue veers toward purple like a freak
& here the young spider lumbers across the clover toward a fallen leaf

Eva's Real-Life Pillowtalk

It itches for a hundred times
I love you for one hundred, that's how much
Do you want to eat five hundred ice creams?
Here.
Be a birddog that flies to the sea, a
    dogbird that flies
Do you want to eat five hundred good-night kisses?
Do you want to eat my good hand?
She advises: you big up eating. "You'll glitter up later," says Jean Day.
There is no time before
There is no time after
"having a daughter"
there is only our daughter-day and our daughter-night
which is why we turn on a light in her room (scare off the dark)
Later, I won't let her see the "monstres en λ" or "à axes parallèles" at the
museum of anatomy. Later, we'll still have a daughter. She'll tell her father:
"It looks like somebody ripped apart the sky then sewed it back together."
Then she'll say:
I wasn't *kicking* you
I was clapping with one foot

Her Yardtalk

"Mamma, how many days do we have
 left to live?" Or did she say,
"Mamma, how many days do we have
 left before we die?"
 This was in the grass in the backyard. I stood up, collecting
 what to say.

my little bird-&-meat subject   little human eye unhinging

Forkhead Box P2 (aka FOXP2)

what haunts the brain: a cell spell

what plush molecules in a cell spell
thought   over the coast of Labrador?

what my mother learned   is in my mind
like a sheet of glass

who go generate a bird's consciousness
who, bees?
who be here sliding on the sheet
of the brain my
brainsheet

who shattering some empathic future

who slice some cerebral cortex   firing in neuropathic pain

who driving Our Lady of the Highways, Susquehanna

The oldest ice on earth has spoken to me
in a brittle, breaking accent

It spoke

the long sad light on the Harlem River
What are these
countries of humans humming What

are they doing here
dancing on the bridge?

The spirit guides of the subterranean parking lot groan —

the self of itself
shine/s in   shine s/in

Come to me

the future comes to me
with a horrifying screech
then it comes to me softly
like a weeping cloud
and it comes to me like
a fish, glass-eyed, flopping
and it comes to me erotically
meanly & sharp
it comes to me cashed out   rolling
            electronically

in my future life I was
a cowboy, killed
in a bar fight

a flamingo in the snow

Bluebottle flies, blue light

        Swallows
with bluebottle flies in their beaks   flew
through the broken window   Thus the neighbor surmised
her neighbor was dead .

[Sit down in the dark theatre. Watch: A love story in which we never
see the woman's face. Are we the lover or are we the beloved? A love
story here in which we are the lover and never see the lover's face.]

even I
have a blue light receptor so
how do I find my way

way out
toward the face
that is my own?

there are waves we see and waves we don't

and a moon clock choreographs coral sex
and a cryptochrome responds in blue light

as if an eye were arrayed on her outer edges
thus a coral's spiny dress is photosensitive to the light
      & dark phases of the moon

a simple Silvereye will read the geomagnetic field

and I will go and I will ply
      for Storm Flooring Co., Inc.

For "there is to be a torch race on horseback for the goddess tonight"

The machine to kiss you

daughter body daughter body
strong & lithe

a flamingo delousing
a flamingo aflame on its
long pink irrevocability

there in front of me in bald
statement, tissue & accusation

How I love more from the mother
How I move more from the mother to the daughter mistaking
        the generic for this specific form :   :

she came to the bed this morning
& put her hands on my breasts
she is the daughter form
what can I say of it
The exchange &
hyphens burrowing

I throw her into the living
and I throw her into the dead
I throw her into the living minute by minute
and would always have her there
how I cast her forward and falling is not my affair   it's the hard work of the body
passing itself along from one minute to the next
I haul her out of the dead word by word
Take the death window out of the body (don't look in)

Take the scalpel out of the hand
Take the word, the dead word, out of the voice
Could she hover in the standing body
always poised on the horizon as an I off-margin, exclamation
to the living Do the living

Dream Event: Face of Time

I am always pressed to the window, a big glass pane at the edge of the movie. We're twin teenagers who must move away from home; we're also a couple at the edge of an upscale used car lot, on the wrong side of the barbed wire. Suddenly, a steel wall rises cubicle-by-cubicle, sealing my twin off from me. I scream. Earlier or later, we're buying a mobile stove/car you can sleep inside, a way to cook and live when you have nowhere: revolutionary technology for the homeless. When I try to light the stove, a 100-foot flame shoots up, spills into an ice fountain, which turns to a frozen pool below us; and soon trapped in the ice right beneath our feet is a woman's beautiful face, huge and digital. The fire is distorting her, she's made of ice crystals of time, each pixilation a minute — a new technology made her; she's wailing: *We've mined the face of time*.

Charlene Dreams

The man was a carcass his meat
spoke

What did it say? It said the Death

of my country speak Speak
to me

I follow a concrete riverbank to find everybody
I will ever know
I will know when I see a party of animals — scattered
around a bend — if all the living
are dead —

I find the whole party of cadaver-like seals — there
we all are — all who have ever lived —
side by side, smiling, the wide river wind-scuffled
the tongue — a piece

of roughened meat — entreats

The Drama of the Shadowdrome

> "'Why is there a shadow there?'
> (making a shadow with the hand)
> Gall (five years old) : *Because there*
> *is a hand.'*
> 'And why is this shadow black?'
> *'Because . . . , because we have bones.'*"

There is the shadow that heals
the shadow that hurts
the shadow that comes from the night

"that's when the child realized that the shadow is not a substance . . . driven
away by light, and learns where a shadow will fall"

My shadow fell on the dirt & rocks as I walked; it did not hurt & I saw
the shadow we open into the ground, shadow-
door down to the dead, my shadow-
        hinge
shadowing my walk back, back down to the shadow family

a pool of blackness puddling in the mind

              Any flower in the garden may
            burst to color and
brought (to) light
the finger leans to describe it
the hand traces light and dark on the page; Dear hand, paint roughly
follow color's instructions

Face my shadow and drop color, drop time
as if the sun (as if the earth) (as if the body)
stopped moving

[I had a dream of keeping the body inside the skull [private territory], shadowless]

there is my shadow on the ground, moving
across death, and there
is my aerial shadow, cast
into bright air (that one is
always invisible)   one is my ghost, one
is my not-ghost shadow

if she put a ring around the man's shadow
I could have slept with this ghost before
If she put a ring around the war
put a ring around the warrior   ring of shadow   *I could have kept that man from war*

like some dark is swallowed by light   some light is swallowed by dark

[body]

stretched toward the lucent wave

when comes "the final adjunct of shine" (Pliny)

Let this me

Let this me, let this you
gather into Charlene   Who is she at the alter
ego   Don't be dumb   she says
the soul salutes the body   poor thing
with its bone pain, hemorrhoids   that's why the soul
keeps its distance   But that's not Charlene
talking   Charlene makes a little hole in the dirt
with her finger   soul's dirt   lets water
pour in   that's how the body gets
so fucking muddy!

Tales from the Geosphere

Then we built roads to tie the earth down tight
    packages of rock & dirt
otherwise the face of the earth
    would have flown right off
    the face of the earth

Houses helped her keep her skirts down

The phrenologist palpates the bumps (earth's skull) —
    clearly a murderer, a patriot
        is housed here, so we knifed & blasted rock & weed, turned the ground
        to a marbled meat territory
From a jet you can still see imprinted on the plains an enormous slaughtered
        boar's snout

Now we'll have to hammer Agamemnon's mask back in place, re-make
the face of the earth   panel by panel   metal by metal   stake it down
with the proper little copper love nails   Pierce
the wormy heart

You look onto the split scene: reality & reality

Essay: The Chinese Shirt / & The Human Body

I wear this Chinese shirt in honor of the human body.

You move toward the bricks.

What moist noises of the deer.

You make shade on the river, a small folded shadow-boat that floats and floats.

Your shadow-finger fingers the tiniest wave.

Strips a leaf in sunlight.

You shoulder another bit of dappled water.

I think of night and exclaim so. It comes out no. Night no.

You thesaurus the fire.
You stoke it, you bank it. The words are
the world, we all know that. But the body
refuses to let go
of the body, seaweed
at its rock clutch. You look onto the split
scene, reality & reality. You are a machine
& you take me
into the cave with tiny robot bears where men & machines teach
men & machines to flay
each other alive. You lead me down
a ramp to escape the destroying world. When we get back every bird
has changed its wing clip, every phoneme has adjusted
its leathers toward a newer color, every restaurant has shifted its menu (lamb

chops are lamp shops), every home has fractioned itself toward a new silk
sidewalk or street. Thank you.   In the new old world order
I'm a time refugee. I will never intercalate the new clock. Prestidigitate me.
You do magic me.
You help me overhear a dream about a 21st birthday with 22 candles
    & you help me
escape from the Chinese buffet. Who are you? You say
buffet *boo-fey*.

We're sitting at a dinner table. I prefer not to recall
the exact company. A few stars dust
themselves across the sky. Put a little gauze on it. I am trying
to ingratiate myself. More stars fly up like a stinging shower. Sparks off the millstone,
daughters of sand & time. You know how to operate the flywheel,
the sun bounces
toward earth & our shoulders glow. I grab someone's hand but it is not someone
I love. Is this the new way to live or
the end of the world?
Back in the house, flesh has been stripped of its bones.
Lightning pulses at the windows like a TV screen licking the glass,
television is trying to enter the house, where we collapse, rubbery, without our bones.

Where have you put my old poetry head?

You point to my old poetry head nestled among the dust. It looks like a chewed-up
rattle or a
stick lying in the corner.

You do all these things, with *opus spicatum*, with ashes, lime, & ammonia. You bleach &
you starch using the ancient methods, you do it for sizing, you preserve the liquid in vats
near the loom weights, you are washing a Roman sheet with lavender seeds, you make
the linens crisp with rhizomic liquids — this is for a trick you will perform later using
teasels and dye fixers.
Hematite for red.

Saffron for yellow.
Woad goes blue.
Alum, lime, & piss near the frigidarium.
Dolia for *garum.*
This is your salted fish factory & you have me.
Do Spanish men ever cry?

They cry golden bone shards in long hollowed cheeks.

You cough radiculopathically & your ligamentum flavum glows.

Oh my myelogram. Here is Our Song:

When it says "fragile" above a body sleeping in the doorway
When it says "fragile" above a body without a home
When it says "fragile" above the exhibit, a pile of bones
You teach me

to clothe a dream in new words
to drape a dream in a new form of words
to put flesh back on the bones and bones back in the body

not *es muerte* but *esta muerte*
because we are not always dead
First we live & *then* we die, processual verb.

A fat girl lighting a crooked cigar.

Using reality goggles, a camera
& a stick
prod the body.
It will leave

in sensory streams. Vision, touch,
balance, body positioned in space
& time

You say, the brain abhors an ambiguity

You say, next is the rubber hand trick
Stroke it with a stick.
Whack it with a hammer
You'll wince
You'll cry out

"The next set of experiments
will involve decoupling
other aspects of sensory embodiment, including
the felt sense of the body
position in space

"and thus
do I [assert] the error that asserts

that one soul on another burns in us"

near Heaven's equator
fragile above the body slum

invaded by [heaven]
drinking a dragon in a cup

Humans, I offer you an angel
for every object on earth, an angel &
the angel's gleaming stream
of piss

this

is how we radiograph the head's history
to revel in/
reveal

Aristotle's true & dirty fingers, the Lord's
long hours

Now to receive your daily ration from a sparrow

make my see-through cherry

my cherry see-through

like a see-through dress
of bones & flesh

made & worn by that witch
of time who teaches
corners to be corners
& rounds to be rounds

You learn a leaf to wiggle a little in wind
a bird learns the ways of the worm
a stick learns to lie still
a man pisses behind a bush

who haunts the
witch of the cherry tree & teaches a tree this:

& if in the hour of death we find ourselves in the same field
get hold of the hay, haywain
hayhead, hey! hell
is to the right

& heaven's there too, a happy
memory ground

Heaven and hell haunt each other
my Master of the Half-Lengths

of light, sewing the eyes
shut then

shouting like a blackbird when the sun comes out an hour

if you want the blood to phosphor
you've got to let the bones phosphor   phosphoresce
throw bright crayons down the veins

don't split   don't slit

    the skin,   human

        of her cherry dress

Coda

I'm wearing a blue-black dress with little silver-lining window-pockets
— our trouble, our
patience, our woe, each of our gifts sewn into its own private pocket

I'm a girl whose name is boy, that's trouble, that's a
pleasure

I phosphoresce near a lemon tree

You could and you did get a new
heart, a not broken
one — see
photograph of not
broken heart with air
pump, yellow & clean
plastic heart   a heart
chamber   chamber with
bright orange dots made
by a German
woman

You put on your bottle-cap coat
made by a man
from Ghana & learn
to make something of what's left
(here on earth)

His Dead Eyebrow (dream event)

Dead dad again, & again the circumstances of his death.
Drunks,   hillside,   darkness,   loss.   Again,
someone who could have helped him but did not. I fear that body may
be me. Father has left a notebook of jibberishy writings, with photos of
his dead self. A close-up of his dead eye like a darkened butterfly. His
dead eyebrow, beautifully arched, horribly bruised.

In waking life (just now), if I read his face like a card there is a reversal
of fortunes, for I am the body he did not help, and when a body dies
we can no longer study the hunger paths so that when I speak of him,
instead of saying "father," I must say "your
father" or "this man I knew" or "this dead man's eyebrow." What is a
dead man? What does a dead man?

Kinesthetic Sketches of the Dead

Someone photographs his hands trembling in black air, radiating electricity & light

Balsa wood configurations are nailed to the legs to show which muscles move as he pedals
These are ghost muscles, limned in calcified lightning.
These are ghost hands, throwing off sparks.
These are ghost bikes.
For my father is always moving through the dark.

(The dead are caught in our studies of motion.)

On the Bus

When I'm not being, I'm not-being
Diving into that vast dark pool   It's
Beautiful   A total sea of nothingness
Is there more something
Or is there more nothing
In the total sum of things?
Some will say
There's no such thing as nothing
But I went swimming there
(foretaste of death)
I say
There's more nothing than something
(it's the most beautiful place in the world)
Not haunting us at the edges of things
But sleeping
Right in the middle of the equipment
Nothing never wakes
though we can be woken from it

Take the scalpel out of the hand

Still Life with Body as Apocalypse

We each drew a picture of the dead man
and each of our pictures looked a little bit more
like the author than the others
my brother around my father's chin
me around my father's speech
my sister around my father's knuckles
the other brother around his habit & waist
We concluded that there's no such thing
as a portrait of a man, just
a portrait of a mob   each
member waiting to see or die themselves

Charlene,

Shall we speak of the dead? How shall we speak of the dead.

www.findagrave.com

when death cradled us

in its shadow,   hugging
        at the edges
                like a baby, kind

    death where
        friends had
                friends & we
            had friends & fathers

84

Charlene said

You can't just throw that piece of salmon back in the river & expect it to swim

The gazelles that rush across the screen will come to an end

(Charlene is eating a pile of oranges in the dark, the door
she sits before is locked — Rainstorm, thunder beyond the windows — she continues —

                about meat that has
        unfound its bones,   thought
            thrown off its earth

a wild worn
to a heap of carcass —)

Teach your flesh to get up off its dish & trot on back —

Like a gazelle before the meteors,
"an open spontaneous animal bleeding its predicaments"

The daughter who is not a shadow of the mother says to the mother:
take your bodies & go —

The body picks up its shadow like a baby and carries it home.

Pauvre fille

I used to be around the poor a lot. My mother
is the poor. Poor Mother. Poor poetry, that cannot
hold her, just as she is, fiddling
in the closets.

the self of itself   shines in

The Tree and the Hill, Epistle

Charlene, here is a landscape or a color & its double [its negative,
its ghost]*
The tree & the hill were haunted
by their words, the words were
haunted by the tree & the hill A word
was carried by a flower The flower
was yellow & was placed on a grave or in a vase There was a point
where they touched Charlene,
what can words see on the other side of themselves? What can
things   This fragile traveler
once asked   and Charlene said

There is no graveyard for words. They kiss the landscape
of real things as they go
What are the disappeared
words Just like the disappeared living But
what is that That
you may never know
        Portrait yourself
                Each human carries her own in-
side feeling of *of*
What happens to the animals who don't
speak English? Speak
Aristotle's Greek or We color
the verbs with our inventions, movements, the landscape
responds (I mean all
animals) Place the yellow in her

*shown by a poet named N

88

hair yellowing
        the place between the flower and
where the mist rises, I mean
an old idea transcendent
heaven   After words
cast their shadow on the hill I can walk
all night and find that place
after the casting, after the hill

or like side-by-side they agree
to meet at some single
points, like silver needles holding
hands, happily piercing
[the landscape & its double] [& its
ghost]

the landscape had a landscape
of words that could be peeled off
& just its silvery seething
spine or skin remained, mercury, the
new transparency
haunted by
haunted by

language was the quarry
where we hunted, where we
mined
turned inside
out, scraped raw
at my word
how might I
see I
don't know
this sleuthy
this sleuth   Uncouth

In the bright & shadowy woods of
representation (kiss kiss) explore
the delicate branchings &
what they carry
past this place
things divide they drift
apart back
toward you
yes
to yellow
that is I do not renounce possi
bility Charlene please who

Dream in which

for Luke

this is a dream in which a male poet left a mean message on the answering machine
and a man I know had died
in which the contents of our cells pushed against their walls
and he was standing on the corner
the life fact shines like loving oil all over the body
and I cried
I was an animal with a past
and we were nastic
in which the Cult of the Moon
and our geonasty kept us moving toward dirt
our photonasty toward light
in which the things on our faithful Earth were dirtied & tired
in which a devotee drove a boat through my heart
this was depicted in 3-D greeting cards with wooden figurines
& it hurt
it hurts
when someone drives a boat through your heart, however small, even in dreams
Men & women & children — what do they have left? A halo
of dirt which is the things of the world worn thin with rubbing

[   ]

Every dream is Charlene
Every sleep fits her ribs just right
            like neoprene
for the big dive

I'd like to deposit my memory banks here
            Sea of Charlene

The Life Fact Shines

Eleni, don't drive so fast

~~~~~~

In my house I have a girl, a funny
little blonde, & a window, take
stock, a rose bush that keeps her
(the soul) from flying off
two legs thus far hold me pinned to the ground
and still ten fingers clacking around
    the cups and plates of the house
In that house, I have a dictionary
of fabulous, ominous words   others
with words in French, in Greek
The words never match up enantiomorphic like two left
hands facing each other *hand la main* το χέρι the outlines are messy
hold up life & life & try to trace them: the moving
shadows and their figurines bleed
which is to say I see   I am not in love with
my objects but I am in love with
their colors I am in love with their
curves but not in love with their
tenacity I hate & love their entropy, bury
the picture in the background, little bird
in the back
yard   the cracked blue cup in the dirt
the mouse the cats dug up
the gutted corpse of the raccoon the new
old moon the gate & the broken door
glass shards in the garden

Travelogue

First we were somewhat Italian, and we sipped espressos on the plazas and watched the pigeons make loops and lunges like thoughts, then we were mostly French, eating hot chocolate with a spoon and reading *Nadja,* then we were more Greek, sipping Nescafés, riding boats to dry and beautiful islands. Soon we were a little bit British, though we knew nothing about it, yet said shove a bum on English couches. We were never Chinese or German but then we read Celan & Goethe & Hölderlin & we were a tiny bit Japanese and took to taking the waters in the mountains outside of small towns in Idaho or having sex with the ex-principals of public junior high schools in the suburbs of Cincinnati, or waking amid goose poop on islands in the Detroit River, not knowing which way was Canadian nor daylight, next we were driving a Chrysler through Kansas and it was summertime, the air conditioning blown out, the long fields of high grasses.

Survey: Phototropes

The snow falls, picks itself up, dusts itself off
a sparrow flying like a leaf back up to its tree
The future does a backbend toward you, it's
what you can almost see, scrimmed
in the clouds that crowd the sky, elbowing, laughing

After that I see space and its influence in a bucket of spinning water
and two calcium atoms shoot forth, twinned photons traveling

back to back, arms unlaced, perfect
swimmers in the lit dusk

Where are they going?

First, to Holland, then
to calcium-kiss her bones

And in Holland the streets are made of water, the dolls & dogs gather
    round lit picnic tables like happy rags

The body is in the root cellar

When snow falls our dead gather close to our bones
because the cold's ghost has come back to haunt the cold & the body
too, is a happy rag

Tree, take a photograph of her thought, you can do it
with photosynthesis: silhouettes of seals appear, a swarmed planet and its
satellites, a celestial atlas that breaks when tapped (it's glass)
Some giraffes, some elephants, a lion scatter
in the clearing; in the clearing

the leaves of the world turn toward the light as do the letters of the word
the words are beautiful not for their accuracy but for their dream:
words-are-arrows that loop between no-man's-land and the wetlands, soft
flints flying toward their target

—words bird the zone—

when home was adopted as mother
area was given here
[a future of] all surface, no border

Acknowledgments

Grateful thanks is given to the following journals and anthologies, and their editors, where some of these poems first appeared:

Conjunctions, Flatmancrooked, Dear Navigator, Bombay Gin, Black Warrior Review, Washington Square, Quarterly West, Cambridge Literary Review (UK), *Poetry International, Trickhouse, Salt Hill, Ping Pong, Poem a Day, The Capilano Review, Clade Song, Juniper 88, Cousin Corinne,* and *The &NOW Awards 2: The Best Innovative Writing.*

"Song: Wake with William" was sung and recorded by Lorna Hunt. It was also performed with Philip Glass and members of the Youth Orchestra of the Americas at the Days & Nights Festival, as was "Shadow Zoo." Thank you to those amazing musicians.

A bow to those who read this manuscript in some of its forms: always Laird Hunt, Tim Atkins, Bill Zaranka for his reading of "The Living Leave the Dead," and for an early reading, Ilya Kaminsky. And to Eva, for providing some really spectacular stuff.

Grace to Susie at Brown Bag Farms, who has changed my life.

I would like to thank the Man Ray Estate for permission to use his deathbed photo of Marcel Proust.

Thank you, Readers, for reading.

Notes

"Bird & Meat Subject" once quoted from Georg Büchner's play *Woyzeck*, and the rock 'n' roll (Nick Cave) production of it directed by Gísli Örn Gardarsson; and from images in the Metropolitan Opera's staging of *Doctor Atomic*.

Sw.t is the Manuel de Codage transliteration of the Egyptian hieroglyphic word for the pitch-black shadow of the soul, which can move independently of its body.

References to a future that is behind us or a past that is before us are inspired by cognitive scientist Rafael Nuñez's reports on the indigenous South American Aymara's "spatial metaphor for chronology," which puts the past in front of us and the future at our backs.

Knockout mice are genetically engineered mice in which a gene has been "knocked out" or turned off.

"[T]he ruthless, splendid labyrinth[s]," comes from Nathalie Angier's article "New Creatures in an Age of Extinctions," *The New York Times*, July 25, 2009.

"An And and Thought" and the last "Charlene said" ("an open spontaneous animal bleeding its predicaments") quote from Eliot Weinberger's translation of Vicente Huidobro's *Altazor*.

"Black-Out Fabric—What I Found There" draws from several reports on "[t]he 'darkest ever' substance known." Using carbon nanotubes, researchers created "the darkest man-made material ever." "[I]t is the closest thing yet to the ideal black material, which absorbs light perfectly at

100

all angles and over all wavelengths." http://news.bbc.co.uk/2/ hi/7190107.stm, reported by Helen Briggs (accessed Jan. 16, 2008).

"Inside the Dome" reworks a line by William Blake; "The Clouds in Heaven," lines from Lucretius in David Slavitt's curious translation (University of California Press, 2008).

"Shadow Zoo" draws freely from Plato's *Republic, Bullfinch's Mythology,* and quotes from www.strategic-air-command.com/missiles/Minuteman/ Minuteman_Missile_History.htm, as well as Jena Osman's *Public Figures* (Wesleyan University Press, 2012). Everyone will see the *Iliad* a few poems later.

"The Humans Attract All the Light of Destiny to Themselves" is part of a sentence from Rachel Bespaloff's essay "On the *Iliad*," translated by Mary McCarthy and published together with Simone Weil's — see below.

"Essay: The Living Leave the Dead," epigram from Simone Weil's "The *Iliad* or the Poem of Force," translated by Mary McCarthy.

"Charlene's binds a Leopard & leads a Mule" and its companion are after Christopher Smart.

Forkhead box P2 (or fox P2) is the gene, located in humans on chromosome 7, thought to control certain language functions in humans and song in birds.

"The Drama of the Shadowdrome" begins with a quote from Piaget's epistemological research in *La causalité physique chez l'enfant (The Child's Conception of Physical Causality).* Many of the shadows in these poems are inspired by Victor I. Stoichita's book *A Short History of the Shadow* (Reaktion, 1997).

Parts of "Essay: The Chinese Shirt / & The Human Body" are inspired by Goya's Black Paintings and by the Roman city below Barcelona.

"His Dead Eyebrow" once contained only a quote of Proust's eye, but Man Ray does not, even in death, allow his photos to be cropped.

The bottom cover image is Étienne-Jules Marey's study of a de Prony brake.

COLOPHON

The Loving Detail of the Living & the Dead
was designed at Coffee House Press,
in the historic Grain Belt Brewery's Bottling House
near downtown Minneapolis. The text is set in Bembo.

FUNDER ACKNOWLEDGMENT

Coffee House Press is an independent, nonprofit literary publisher. Our books are made possible through the generous support of grants and gifts from many foundations, corporate giving programs, state and federal support, and through donations from individuals who believe in the transformational power of literature. Coffee House Press receives major operating support from Amazon, the Bush Foundation, the Jerome Foundation, the McKnight Foundation, from Target, and in part from a grant provided by the Minnesota State Arts Board through an appropriation by the Minnesota State Legislature from the State's general fund and its arts and cultural heritage fund with money from the vote of the people of Minnesota on November 4, 2008, and a grant from the Wells Fargo Foundation of Minnesota. Support for this title was received from the National Endowment for the Arts, a federal agency. Coffee House also receives support from: several anonymous donors; Suzanne Allen; Elmer L. and Eleanor J. Andersen Foundation; Around Town Agency; Patricia Beithon; Bill Berkson; the E. Thomas Binger and Rebecca Rand Fund of the Minneapolis Foundation; the Patrick and Aimee Butler Family Foundation; Ruth Dayton; Dorsey & Whitney, LLP; Mary Ebert and Paul Stembler; Chris Fischbach and Katie Dublinski; Fredrikson & Byron, P.A.; Sally French; Anselm Hollo and Jane Dalrymple-Hollo; Jeffrey Hom; Carl and Heidi Horsch; Alex and Ada Katz; Stephen and Isabel Keating; the Kenneth Koch Literary Estate; Kathy and Dean Koutsky; the Lenfestey Family Foundation; Carol and Aaron Mack; Mary McDermid; Sjur Midness and Briar Andresen; the Nash Foundation; the Rehael Fund of the Minneapolis Foundation; Schwegman, Lundberg & Woessner, P.A.; Kiki Smith; Jeffrey Sugerman; Patricia Tilton; the Archie D. & Bertha H. Walker Foundation; Stu Wilson and Mel Barker; the Woessner Freeman Family Foundation; Margaret and Angus Wurtele; and many other generous individual donors.

To you and our many readers across the country,
we send our thanks for your continuing support.

MISSION

The mission of Coffee House Press is to publish exciting, vital, and enduring authors of our time; to delight and inspire readers; to contribute to the cultural life of our community; and to enrich our literary heritage. By building on the best traditions of publishing and the book arts, we produce books that celebrate imagination, innovation in the craft of writing, and the many authentic voices of the American experience.

VISION

LITERATURE. We will promote literature as a vital art form, helping to redefine its role in contemporary life. We will publish authors whose groundbreaking work helps shape the direction of 21st-century literature.

WRITERS. We will foster the careers of our writers by making long-term commitments to their work, allowing them to take risks in form and content.

READERS. Readers of books we publish will experience new perspectives and an expanding intellectual landscape.

PUBLISHING. We will be leaders in developing a sustainable 21st-century model of independent literary publishing, pushing the boundaries of content, form, editing, audience development, and book technologies.

VALUES

Innovation and excellence in all activities

Diversity of people, ideas, and products

Advancing literary knowledge

Community through embracing many cultures

Ethical and highly professional management
and governance practices

Join us in our mission at coffeehousepress.org

ELENI SIKELIANOS is the author of six previous books of poetry, most recently *Body Clock* and *The California Poem;* the hybrid memoir, *The Book of Jon;* and a translation of Jacques Roubaud's *Exchanges on Light.* She has been the happy recipient of awards from the National Endowment for the Arts, the Fulbright Foundation, the National Poetry Series, and the New York Foundation for the Arts, among others, and of Princeton University's Seeger Fellowship and two Gertrude Stein Awards for Innovative American Writing. Sikelianos's work has been widely anthologized, in two Norton anthologies (*Postmodern American Poetry* and *American Hybrid*) as well as Tin House's *Satellite Convulsions, A Best of Fence,* and *The Arcadia Project.* She has collaborated with filmmakers, visual artists, composers, and musicians, including Philip Glass and Ed Bowes. At present, she teaches in and directs the Creative Writing Program at the University of Denver and teaches for Naropa's Summer Writing Program. She shares her days with the novelist Laird Hunt and their daughter Eva Grace.

ELENI SIKELIANOS RECOMMENDS
THESE COFFEE HOUSE PRESS BOOKS

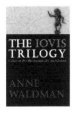

The Iovis Trilogy, by Anne Waldman
978-1-56689-255-1
"A book to admire, to pay homage to, to get lost in, Waldman's epic goes splendidly on and on, mixing the shamanistic with the diaristic, the topical with the prayerful, incorporating almost everything."—*Publishers Weekly*, starred review
2012 PEN Center USA Literary Award for Poetry

The Green Lake Is Awake, by Joseph Ceravolo
978-1-56689-021-2
"This valuable contribution to American poetics restores Ceravolo's boldly asyntactic yet stunningly precise work to book form. . . . His work, blending the sound-sculpting of a Clark Coolidge with deceptively calm, Ashbery-like meditations, carries within it an original and bewitching prosody as delicate as anything in Hopkins."—*Publishers Weekly*

Necessary Distance, by Clarence Major
978-1-56689-109-7
"Major, one of America's most gifted and versatile writers, continues to engage the reading public with his innovative fiction and poetry. In remarks that are lively and enthusiastic, Major discusses such authors as Paul Laurence Dunbar, the first black poet to draw heavily upon African folk models; Wallace Thurman, a precocious early novelist who argued in favor of aesthetic freedom for black writers; and Claude McKay, a native Jamaican whose works are strongly associated with the Harlem Renaissance."—**ELLEN SULLIVAN**, *Library Journal*

A Handmade Museum, by Brenda Coultas
978-1-56689-143-1
"Following Mina Loy's footsteps to the dumpsters of the Bowery, New York poet Coultas works in public: 'I write poems for twenty, that's twenty people to a poem.' In these five sets of poems, Coultas unearths an entire America, 'Buffaloville/ Newtonville/ Yankeeville/Patronville.'"
—*Publishers Weekly*
2004 The Poetry Society of America's Norma Farber First Book Award Winner